THE SIMON & GARFUNKEL COLLECTION

S0-AAZ-560

Published by
Wise Publications
14-15 Berners Street, London W1T 3LJ, UK.

Exclusive Distributors:
Music Sales Limited
Distribution Centre, Newmarket Road, Bury St.Edmunds, Suffolk IP33 3YB, UK.
Music Sales Corporation
257 Park Avenue South, New York, NY 10010, USA.
Music Sales Pty Limited
20 Resolution Drive, Caringbah, NSW 2229, Australia.

Order No. PS10776
ISBN 0-7119-0064-7
This book © Copyright Wise Publications,
a division of Music Sales Limited.

Unauthorised reproduction of any part of this publication by any
means including photocopying is an infringement of copyright.

Your Guarantee of Quality
As publishers, we strive to produce every book
to the highest commercial standards. This book has been
carefully designed to minimise awkward page turns
and to make playing from it a real pleasure.
Particular care has been given to specifying acid-free, neutral-sized paper
made from pulps which have not been elemental chlorine bleached. This pulp is from
farmed sustainable forests and was produced with special regard for the environment.
Throughout, the printing and binding have been planned to ensure
a sturdy, attractive publication which should give years of enjoyment.
If your copy fails to meet our high standards, please inform us
and we will gladly replace it.

www.musicsales.com

I AM A ROCK

Words and music by Paul Simon

Slowly

©1965 Paul Simon. All Rights Reserved. International Copyright Secured.

HOMEWARD BOUND

Words and music by Paul Simon

Moderately

1. I'm sit - tin' in the rail - way sta - tion, got a tick - et for my
2. Ev - 'ry day's an end - less stream___ of cig - a - rettes and
(3. To -) night I'll sing my songs a - gain,___ I'll play the game

dest - in - a - tion. _____ Mm _____
mag - a - zines. _____ Mm _____
and pre - tend. _____ Mm _____

© 1966 Paul Simon. All Rights Reserved. International Copyright Secured.

On a tour of one night stands my suit-case and gui-tar
And each town looks the same to me, the mov-ies and the fac-
But all my words come back to me in shades of me-di-oc-

in hand and ev-'ry stop is neat-ly planned for a
-tor-ies and ev-'ry strang-er's face I see re-
-ri-ty like emp-ti-ness in har-mon-ny I

po-et and a one man band.
minds me that I long to be,
need some-one to com-fort me.

Chorus:

Home-ward Bound, I wish I was,

7

Home - ward ___ Bound. Home where my thought's_

___ es - cap - ing, Home where my mu - sic's play - ing, Home where my love_

___ lies wait - ing si - lent - ly for me. ___ 3. To-

Si - lent - ly for me. ___

THE 59th STREET BRIDGE SONG
(FEELIN' GROOVY)

Words and music by Paul Simon

© 1966 Paul Simon. All Rights Reserved. International Copyright Secured.

look-in' for fun and Feel - in' Groov - y. _____

Hel - lo lamp - post, what - cha know - in' I've come to watch your flow -

- ers grow - in'. Ain't - cha got no rhymes ___ for me?

Doot - in' doo - doo, Feel - in' Groov - y. _____ Got

10

AMERICA

Words and music by Paul Simon

© 1968 Paul Simon. All Rights Reserved. International Copyright Secured.

I said, "Be care - ful, His bow - tie is real - ly a cam - 'ra."___

"Toss me a cig - a - rette, I think there's

one in my rain - coat."___

field.

"Kath - y, I'm lost I said, Though I knew she was

sleep - ing. _____ I'm emp - ty and

ach - ing and I don't ___ know why." _____

Count - ing the cars On the New Jer - sey Turn - pike. They've all

come _____ to look for A - mer _____ - i -

ca, _____ All come _____ to

Repeat and fade.

look for A - mer - i - ca. _____

WEDNESDAY MORNING 3 A.M.

Words and music by Paul Simon

Moderately bright

1. I can hear the soft breath-ing of the girl that I love,
2. (She is) soft, she is warm, but my heart re-mains

heav-y, As she lies here be-side me a-
heav-y, And I watch as her breasts gent-ly

© 1966 Paul Simon. All Rights Reserved. International Copyright Secured.

I held up and robbed __ a hard   liq - uor
The morn - ing is

store. _____

4. My

just   a   few   hou - - - rs _____   a -

way. _____

EL CONDOR PASA (IF I COULD)

English Lyric by Paul Simon
Musical arrangement by J. Milchberg and D. Robles

© 1933, 1963, 1970 Edward B. Marks Music Corporation and Jorge Milchberg.
English lyric © 1970 Charing Cross Music, Inc.
All Rights Reserved. International Copyright Secured.

way,   I'd rath - er sail a - way____   Like a swan   that's here and gone.   A

man   gets tied up to the ground,   He gives the world   its sad-dest sound,   its sad-dest

sound.____   I'd rath-er be a for-est than a

street.   Yes I would.   If I could,____   I sure-ly would.____   I'd

rath-er feel the earth be-neath my feet. Yes I would. If I on-ly

could,_____ I sure-ly would._____

AT THE ZOO

Words and music by Paul Simon

© 1967 Paul Simon. All Rights Reserved. International Copyright Secured.

an - i - mals will love it, if___ you do, _____ if you

do. _____ Oo _____ Oo _____

Some-thing tells me, it's all hap-pen-ing At The Zoo.___

I do be-lieve___ it, ___ I do be-lieve__ it's true.___

SCARBOROUGH FAIR (CANTICLE)

Words and music by Paul Simon

Moderately slow

Are you go-ing _____ to Scar - bor-ough Fair: _____

_____ Pars - ley, sage, rose - mar - y and

© 1966 Paul Simon. All Rights Reserved. International Copyright Secured.

On the side of a hill in the deep for - est
On the side of a hill a sprink - ling of
War bel - lows blaz - ing in scar - let bat -

Tell her to make me a cam - bric shirt: _____
Tell her to find me an a - cre of land: _____
Tell her to reap it with a sick - le of leath - er: _____

green.
leaves.
tal - ions.

Trac - ing of spar - row on
Wash - es the grave with
Gen - er - als or - der their

Pars - ley, sage, rose - mar - y and thyme; _____
Pars - ley, sage, rose - mar - y and thyme; _____
Pars - ley, sage, rose - mar - y and thyme; _____

snow - crest - ed brown.
sil - ver - y tears.
sol - diers to kill.

Blan - kets and
A sol - dier
And to fight for a

With - out no seams nor nee - dle
Be - tween the salt wa - ter and the sea
And gath - er it all in a bunch of

THE BOXER

Words and music by Paul Simon

Moderate tempo

I am just a poor boy. Though my sto-ry's sel-dom told, I have squan-dered my re-sis-tance for a pock-et-ful of mum-bles, such are prom-is-es.

© 1968 Paul Simon. All Rights Reserved. International Copyright Secured.

no more than a boy in the com-pa-ny of stran-gers in the

qui-et of a rail-way sta-tion run-ning scared, _____

Lay-ing low, seek-ing out the poor-er quar-ters where the

rag-ged peo-ple go, Look-ing for the plac-es on-ly they would

THE SOUND OF SILENCE

Words and music by Paul Simon

 © 1964 Paul Simon. All Rights Reserved. International Copyright Secured.

A HAZY SHADE OF WINTER

Words and music by Paul Simon

Moderate tempo

Time, time,— time,——— See what's be - come of me,——————————— while I———

——— looked a - round   for my— pos - si - bil - i - ties,————— I was so

© 1966 Paul Simon. All Rights Reserved. International Copyright Secured.

MRS. ROBINSON

Words and music by Paul Simon

© 1968 Paul Simon. All Rights Reserved. International Copyright Secured.

God bless you, please, Mrs.— Rob - in - son,— Heav-en holds— a place—

— for those who pray, _____ (Hey, hey, hey,_____

— hey, hey, hey. _____)

Verse:
1. We'd like to know a lit - tle bit a - bout— you for our files,—

D.S. al Coda

Coda

Verse:

G

G7

2. Hide it in a hid - ing place __ where
3. Sit - ting on a so - fa on __ a

no one ev - er goes, _____
Sun - day af - ter - noon, _____

C7

Put it in your pan - try with __ your cup - cakes, _____
Go - ing to the can - di - dates' __ de - bate, _____

F7

Bb

It's a lit - tle se - cret, just __ the Rob -
Laugh a - bout it, shout __ a - bout __ it,

KEEP THE CUSTOMER SATISFIED

Words and music by Paul Simon

Moderately bright

Gee but it's great to be back home,
Dep - u - ty Sher - iff said to me

Home is where I want to
Tell me what you come here

be. _____
for, _____ boy.

I've been on the road so long my friend,
You bet - ter get your bags and flee.

And if you came a - long I know you could - n't dis - a - gree. ____
You're in trou - ble boy, And now you're head - ing in - to more. ____

© 1970 Paul Simon. All Rights Reserved. International Copyright Secured.

It's the same old story_____ (Yeah) Ev-'ry-where I

It's the same old sto-ry_____

go,_____ I get slan-dered, Li-beled,_____ I hear words_____

I nev-er heard in the Bi-ble._____ And I'm one step a-head of the

shoe shine, Two steps a-way from the coun-ty line, Just trying to keep my cus-tom-ers

sat - is - fied, Sat - is - fied. _____ fied. _____

Woh _____ Woh _____ Woh _____ Woh _____

_____ But it's the same old

sto - ry _____ Ev - 'ry-where I go, _____ I get

SONG FOR THE ASKING

Words and music by Paul Simon

Here is my Song For The Ask-ing, Ask me and I will play so sweet-ly, I'll make you smile; This is my tune for the tak-ing, Take it, don't turn a-way I've been

© 1970 Paul Simon. All Rights Reserved. International Copyright Secured.

CECILIA

Words and music by Paul Simon

Moderate, not too fast, rhythmically

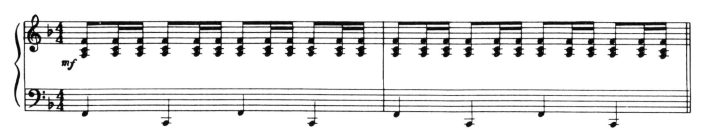

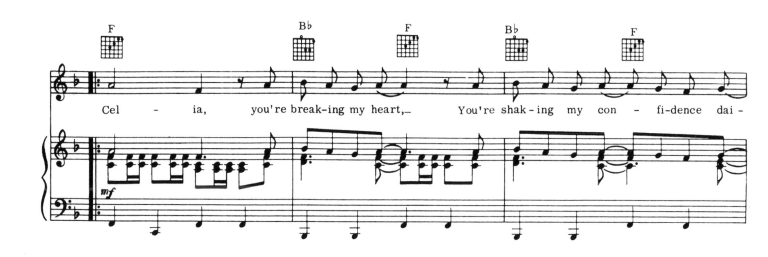

Cel - ia, you're break-ing my heart,_ You're shak-ing my con - fi-dence dai-

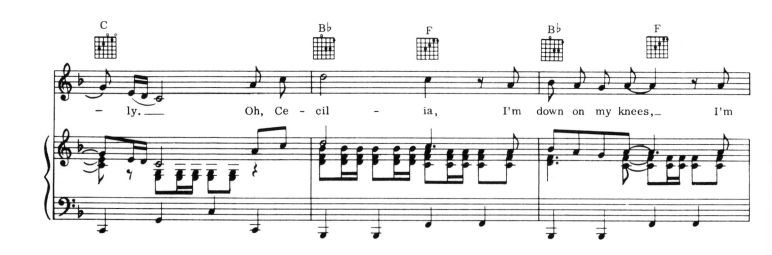

- ly.___ Oh, Ce - cil - ia, I'm down on my knees,_ I'm

© 1969 Paul Simon. All Rights Reserved. International Copyright Secured.

BOOKENDS

Words and music by Paul Simon

 © 1968 Paul Simon. All Rights Reserved. International Copyright Secured.

Long a-go it must be   I have a pho-to-graph___ Pre-serve your mem-o-ries;___ They're all that's left you.

OLD FRIENDS

Words and music by Paul Simon

 © 1968 Paul Simon. All Rights Reserved. International Copyright Secured.

BRIDGE OVER TROUBLED WATER

Words and music by Paul Simon

© 1969 Paul Simon. All Rights Reserved. International Copyright Secured.

I'm on your side. _____ Oh,—
I'll take your part. _____ Oh,—

— when times_ get rough _____ And friends just can't be found,—
— when dark-ness comes__ And pain is all a - round,—

Like a Bridge O - ver Trou-bled Wa - ter

I will lay me down. Like a Bridge O - ver Trou-bled Wa - ter

Sail on sil-ver girl, Sail on by. Your time has come to shine.— All your dreams are on their way. See how they shine._____ Oh,— if you need a friend

Bringing you the words and the music

All the latest music in print... rock & pop plus jazz, blues, country, classical and the best in West End show scores.

- Books to match your favourite CDs.

- Book-and-CD titles with high quality backing tracks for you to play along to. Now you can play guitar or piano with your favourite artist... or simply sing along!

- Audition songbooks with CD backing tracks for both male and female singers for all those with stars in their eyes.

- Can't read music? No problem, you can still play all the hits with our wide range of chord songbooks.

- Check out our range of instrumental tutorial titles, taking you from novice to expert in no time at all!

- Musical show scores include *The Phantom Of The Opera*, *Les Misérables*, *Mamma Mia* and many more hit productions.

- DVD master classes featuring the techniques of top artists.

It's Easy To Play New Chart Hits

Recorder Wizard

THE ESSENTIAL COLLECTION CLASSICAL GOLD

Classic Masterclass Series THE BEATLES MASTER SESSION

HITS OF THE YEAR

CHART HITS NOW! HOW WE DO (PARTY)

THE ESSENTIAL COLLECTION HANDEL GOLD

Now! Volume 2 Guitar Tab WHITE PAGES

Matilda

LED ZEPPELIN

Visit your local music shop or, in case of difficulty, contact the Marketing Department, Music Sales Limited, Newmarket Road, Bury St Edmunds, Suffolk, IP33 3YB, UK marketing@musicsales.co.uk